Hearing from Heaven

Elaine Marie Keane

Hearing from Heaven
Copyright © 2025 by Elaine Marie Keane

ISBN: 979-8894791678 (sc)

The Reading Glass Books
1-888-420-3050
www.readingglassbooks.com
production@readingglassbooks.com

DEDICATION

This book of visions is dedicated to the Holy Spirit, God the Father, and His beautiful son Christ Jesus or the Holy Trinity. They receive all the honor and credit for these visions. In scripture it says, I can of myself do nothing, but with Christ I can do all things (Phil. 4:13).

Contents

Seeing *and* Talking *with* Jesus

Book 1

Part I

The Training Of A Prophet.

In early childhood I learned a song called, "Jesus loves me, this I know, for the bible tells me so little ones to him belong they are weak but He is strong." This song of worship opened up an intimacy with the Lord. Later in my life, Jesus told me we have been talking with one another since I was two years of age. This talking with the Lord started when He was feeling compassion for a young girl child whose parents were soon getting a divorce. All attention was being delivered to her newborn baby sister from everyone in her surroundings. The young girl was lonely and not feeling loved by anyone so she turned to Jesus and received the love and attention she needed. She learned Jesus does love her.

Later while playing in a garden of blooming peonies in May, after just turning six years old, I met and talked with Jesus. Jesus asked me to help Him save my family and others, but mainly my family. I told Him that I would because I loved Him, and even at this age I could tell how much Jesus loved me in return.

Many years later Jesus allowed me to have fifty saved souls. This came about through an active prayer life as an intercessor. These fifty souls were listed and prayed for, they were my family and friends. Jesus promised me He saved them all, even though one was in Hell. After listening to many Biblical teachings about saving souls and feeling bad because I had not directly saved any souls, Jesus helped me. I had contributed to other ministries who were saving souls to present to the Lord, but I wanted to have saved souls to present to Jesus when I went to Heaven.

I wanted to do what He told me to do when I was six. He asked me to help Him save my family and others.

When about eight years of age, I was staying with my grand- parents on their farm. We witnessed a miracle of lights I will never forget. At sunrise the sun was a faint white ball, but all around the sun was a cloudless sky, that started turning colors of the rainbow. An example the sky turned from lavender to pink, then to peach, then to deep yellow, then to green, to blue and back to lavender. I have never witnessed anything like this again. I understand God loved my grandparents and He was showing His love to them for my grandparents had loved God all their lives.

When about twelve years of age, God called me out loud three times. My mother told me to say "speak Lord thy servant is listening" at the third calling. I did not realize the significance of this until years later.

After this time life became very busy with finishing junior high and high school, then college, then learning how to be an art teacher, then marriage to a wonderful man finally. I had two children by the time I was thirty-four.

At thirty-six while watching the 700 Club with Pat Robertson and praying with him, I received a spontaneous baptism of the Holy Spirit and received the gift of tongues. The gift of tongues I received was a supernatural gift of a Heavenly, unknown language. Some people receive a known language of the Earth that they don't speak. This is a gift of the Holy Spirit to show you that you indeed have been baptized and received the Holy Spirit. Also, the more you pray in tongues, the faster they come and can get more diverse or multiple languages. My body also shook and my hands trembled praying or practicing the Holy Spirit baptism similar to the Quakers who shook and trembled praying or practicing the present of God when the Holy Spirit filled them! Then I attended classes in the charismatic movement of the baptism in the Holy Spirit in the Catholic Church and was infilled more deeply and received rebaptism. I asked the Holy Spirit for the gift of prophecy and pretty pictures to see and paint since I was an art teacher and painter. He gave me open visions-eyes open and closed visions - eyes closed. Open eye visions and closed eye visions occur when God starts using our eyes, since the eyes are the windows of the soul. In an open eye visions our eyes are open and we see the physical reality before them, but superimposed over the reality picture is a spiritual picture which seems to be bigger and brighter and also there is a message God is trying to give us. In closed eye visions, our eyes are closed and we see a giant movie being played out in the front of our minds. The movie tells a story or as message from the Lord God.

God has a fantastic sense of humor and gave me the gift of prophecy in visual form or visions. Since then I have painted visions. Jesus told me you can paint pictures (visions) with words as well as paint pictures on canvas. Good to know for an art teacher and a prophet. Now I know why he called me when I was younger.

Because this gift of visual prophecy was different than other prophets and their prophecies in this charismatic group, I made them (other prophets) uncomfortable and I went through a little persecution. Prophets are supposed to judge the prophecy made by other prophets or judge any prophecy spoken in the church to make sure it is the truth. I was told at first I could not give any prophecy at all, then they changed their minds and said I could give prophecy in speech but not the picture vision, Then I was told to only give the picture vision I have received and speak nothing about this picture vision. After trying to comply with their requests I gave up and left the charismatic group. Because I was so hurt by this persecution I decided never to give prophecy again. But praise the Lord the Holy Spirit showed me His compassion in a beautiful vision to take away the hurt and encourage me.

I was lying on my bedroom floor face down crying, then the Holy Spirit sent by Jesus appeared as a very large dove and enclosed me in His wings and comforted me with His love. The dove was beautiful, covered in diamonds and pearls. I tried to paint this but could not begin to show the beauty of the Holy Spirit Dove. All seers are prophets but all prophets aren't seers I learned.

Years later, God showed me another high cut sapphire stone and on the surface of the stone was superimposed the face of Jesus. The Holy Spirit gives me a lot of information with the visions and the Holy Spirit speaks with me when I pray and practice His presence. He told me blue was God's favorite color.

Part II

Speaking Visions of Jesus Often Called Vision Speaking by Other Prophets.

During the funeral service in a Catholic church, Jesus showed me a vision of the departed (a relative) at the front of the church with Him. Jesus said to the departed, "See how much they loved you!" The most important thing was how much Jesus loved the departed and that the departed was with Jesus forever. What I experienced during the funeral was an open vision.

The whole day had been cloudy and rainy, but all of a sudden a stream of radiant light came through the stained-glass window in the front of the church. The light rays hit the casket of the departed. Jesus showed His love for all the people in the church who were grieving. Needless to say, this affected me deeply and I cried like a baby to see that much of His love for the departed and the people grieving.

Once while making the communion bread for a Bible group, Jesus showed me a vision of Himself holding up in one hand the communion bread representing His body and in His other hand a cup of wine representing His blood. This vision was later painted. I gave the painting to a Christian friend.

In another vision painted of Jesus it looked like Jesus was standing in a very blue sky with a ring of bright white light sur- rounding Him. There are also streams of intense light going through every wound He received to save us. There were light rays representing the crown of thorns around His head. There were intense rays of lights coming from His hands and feet where He had been nailed to the cross. A big ray of light came from His side where the lance hit him and a large intense ray of light coming from His heart. This vision reminds us to be in awe of Jesus. This painting was given to another Christian.

Another vision was of the crown of thorns with big white Easter lilies interwoven in the crown of thorns. The lilies represent purity endured and the thorns represent the persecution He endured for us on the cross. Jesus was the perfect, pure man who died for us because no earthly man could do this to remove our sin.

Later Jesus showed a vision which became another painting. Jesus was holding the bride (His church) in His arms. The bride was looking at the holes in His hands and crying because she could see the love Jesus had for His bride so that He was able to endure the cross for her. Jesus was endowed with light all around Him and He had on a red sash over His white robe. The bride also had on a red sash over her white robe because of what He did for her. He made her like Him. This vision became a painting.

Once after enduring a very intense summer storm, Jesus showed me a vision of Him walking through dark clouds and breaking them up. His robe matched the light showing around the clouds and in His hand was a rainbow that arched over Him to show coming light around Him and departure of the dark clouds and breaking up of the storm. Later Jesus showed me how we can control weather by praying prayers to break up storms before they get to us or breaking in half and going around us.

TRAINING A PROPHET

As a young girl I was swinging on my new swing set. I was swinging with my head thrown back and looking up at the sky. All of a sudden Jesus showed me a vision of me walking up a series of clouds into Heaven. The clouds started with the biggest cloud near me then each cloud in a row got smaller and smaller as they ascended into the sky. The clouds were actually there in the sky but Jesus allowed me to see me walking up the clouds like a ladder into His Heavenly home.

The sky was very blue and the clouds were golden and the only clouds in the sky.

I was told by my mother when I was growing up of being fey she meant able to see into the future a visionary, being of Scott Irish descent.

Part III

Protection of Jesus

When in college a group of friends went to a national park in the mountains for a swim and picnic. We were in a hurry to return to school in order to meet a sign in deadline. The driver was not use to driving in the mountains due to being raised in a flat beach area. Jesus warned me we were going to hit a tree on the side of the road. I was scared and I fainted my body became completely lax. When I woke up, we had hit a tree and I was the only one in the car uninjured because I was unconscious during the wreck. I did not even feel the car hit the tree. No one was seriously hurt but we all spent the night in the hospital. Most of us were released the next day and went back to school or to work.

Later when married and with two children, we were going on vacation to Florida to take the kids to Disneyworld. We were in South Carolina and God showed me a vision of a white truck with a big blue stripe that would hit (wreck) us in Jacksonville Florida before we could turn west to go to Orlando. I took this vision and warning seriously and asked for God's mercy. After praying in tongues for a long while we proceeded to Jacksonville, Florida. When we got there, we saw the white truck with the blue stripe but it did not hit us, we got to Disneyworld with no problem. Praise the Lord for His protection.

After being an intercessor and praying for this country for forty years to have a great spiritual awakening and finally getting my minister's license after taking religious courses for years, I was pursued by witches and warlocks trying to stop me. I told the Lord I was weary of the pursuit of evil ones everywhere I went. They were always trying to destroy me, deceive me or kill me. When Satan is worried that someone might affect his kingdom or power he sends his followers to persecute.

But this has mostly stopped now. I was in a store buying art supplies and three warlocks were there. I heard one warlock say to his wife that he could not do anything to persecute me or stop me. I think it was because the warlock realized I was in my spiritual armor and protected by Jesus. Greater is He that is within me than he that is in the world. All occurred for ten years after I received my ministering license.

Jesus said I would be hid in Him, in His light and be protected because darkness cannot enter light or it can't penetrate His Holy light. The enemy will only see my light, they will not see you, when you are in me no evil can hurt you. Greater is He that is within me than he that is in the world. Darling you are within me and I am within you, no evil can destroy you, you are mine.

He showed me another vision of Him as a light being opening His robe and taking me a little being tucking me into under His robe and then recovering me. They can't find you, for you are hidden in my light and under my blood. When evil ones say curses toward you the curses will return to the evil ones and they will destroy themselves with the words of their own mouths. They will learn quickly not to do this.

Jesus has shown me two visions of my spiritual armor. One was of a little dress made up of strings of pearls at the top and at the bottom of the dress. The pearls were made by the oysters to sur- round an irritant to it, the pearls keep out Satan the irritant.

The other vision was of my spiritual armor which was made up of armor made up of diamonds, a hard substance. My loins were girt about with a girdle of diamonds (truth) my breastplate was a big diamond covering (righteousness) my feet were shod with big diamond boots (preparation of the Gospel of peace - I had a huge diamond shield of faith, a helmet made of a huge diamond (Helmet of salvation) and a sword of the spirit which was also formed out of a diamond. I put on my spiritual armor every day.

Jesus not only protects His loved ones but also protects Israel. He showed me a vision of Jesus holding up a very exhausted Israeli soldier in one arm pushing back the enemies of Israel with His other arm, warning them to leave Israel alone. The soldier was holding up an Israeli flag and both were superimposed over the State of Israel.

This vision was received when Israel was fighting off many Muslim nations around it.

A painting was made of this vision and given to an Israeli friend, to remind her of how much Jesus loves Israel and Israel will always come out on top because of this loving protection. I will bless those who bless you and curse those who curse you (Genesis 12:3).

Jesus showed me a vision of Donald Trump and Prime Minister Benjamin Netanyahu walking together with Jesus between the two. Trump was on one side of Jesus and Netanyahu was on the other side of Jesus. Jesus had an arm thrown over the shoulders of each man. They were walking together in agreement, all stepping for- ward on the same leg in time with one another. This vision was sur- rounded with the light of Jesus. Jesus approves of this friendship. When doing something Satan is worried about I've seen visions of him pointing an accusing finger at me. I've seen this vision twice and I know he was trying to scare me. Jesus grabbed him by his accusing finger, wound him around and around then pitched him into Hell. Thank you for your protection Jesus.

Jesus has shown me many visions of Heaven but there is Hell also. One of the best books written about Hell being very real was by Mary K. Baxter called a Divine Revelation of Hell. Jesus took Mary K. Baxter to Hell for many nights and showed her all the different parts of hell. Jesus talked with hell's captives and they pleaded to get out, but they were in hell because of their decision or their will. I want my decision and will to be in Heaven with Jesus.

HEALING LOVE OF JESUS

I was diagnosed with breast cancer when forty years of age. I had two small children, four and five and I begged Jesus to let me stay long enough on earth to raise up my children. Jesus told me He was healing me of cancer and that I would never have it again as long as I lived. He also told me not to believe Satan if he told me I was getting cancer again, I was to remind Satan what Jesus told me. I have been cancer free for 39 years since then.

Part IV

The Love of Jesus

Jesus says you can brush pictures with words and visions. Jesus showed me a vision of Him with a big paint brush. He was painting us with love, anointing, faith and light. Go into the world and paint His light in a dark world. Paint His love and anointing wherever you go.

In a prophetic dream I saw me using my sword of the spirit (the sword was bright like diamonds). I was in a dark vista, fighting in darkness. The sword turned into a big paint brush bright like diamonds in the dark vista. I was fighting with a big paint brush of Jesus' love. It changed all the people it touched to be like Jesus. Praise the Lord.

Jesus kisses the face of first believer, He loves all of us but some believers do not spend the time with Jesus in order to be truly intimate with Him. The next believer does spend time with Jesus and shows his love to Jesus. This is why the kiss on the mouth. It shows a deeper love for Jesus even while we are in a physical form here on Earth, a more Eden experience.

Speaking in tongues and diamonds coming out of mouth. God is showing believer diamonds are beautiful and are known for their strength. Tongues are beautiful because they are the answer to many problems we face. They are the answers from Heaven and give us the strength we need in times of trouble.

Jesus shows a vision of Him exchanging hearts with me. Jesus put His heart in my chest, He takes my heart and puts it into His chest. Now I have a cross on my heart as well as Jesus has a cross on His heart.

Part V

Visions About Country USA

Destructive weather caused by destructive people. There are many signs of destructive weather, hurricanes, tornadoes, tsunamis, fires and floods. We also have earthquakes and volcanoes. This year we had Florence and Michael. This Earth is distressed and grieving because of the sin on the Earth. The Earth was made for Eden, perfect, good men and God. Christians are holding the Earth together literally.

During the Old Testament times, no one but the High Priest was allowed into the Holy of Holies but once a year, in order to place a blood sacrifice on the Ark of the testimony or the mercy seat. Jesus showed me a vision twice of His mercy towards me. I was enfolded by the wings of the angels on the mercy seat because I was going through troublesome times! This amazed me and the only way it was possible was because of the blood sacrifice of Jesus for us. We can have a relationship with God the father with no fear.

There is no global warming, there is only global sin warming. The Town of Paradise in California was burned completely to the ground by Satanic fire reminding me of Hell. Even man's paradise can burn, we must turn to God.

I had a vision of two water ducts, both are clogged. God removes clogged duct of sin in the USA. The other duct is obstruction in my life and your life and God is clearing sin directed at you and me and your personal sin. This is called redemption! This vision was received in intercessory prayer before church took place in the year of 2016. My visions are given to me from Jesus via the Holy Spirit. Usually when God shows me an open vision, it is very important to receive the information. When I receive a closed vision I am usually praying in the presence of Jesus.

Jesus told me the only reason our money still works is because (In God We Trust) is still printed on it. Sin in country opened up the way to destructive weather and destructive people.

Saw an American flag up close. A lot of American Christians are still praying for America even though America has not followed Him, God still honors the prayers of the ones who do love him.

If my people, who are called by my name will humble them- selves and turn from their wicked ways, then I will hear their prayers and heal their land.

Jesus showed me two visions on September 21, 2014. It was a picture vision of a watering can sprinkling a flat map of the land in USA. This is a natural (rain) as well as a supernatural sprinkling of water over USA. This is to fix natural draught but also spiritual draught. When drops of water hit land, inside the drops were people praising God with hands and arms raised in worship.

The next vision was of wind blowing away dry dust or dirt and sin. Then radiant light comes down and strikes land from Heaven. "Because my people and intercessors have been praying to me to forgive their land and heal it of sin, I will remove the sin debt and cover the land with new light of my love and grace and mercy." (Chronicles 7:14) God told me this when I was praying for this country. When I sit quietly and listen, God will talk to me and tell me things of the future. This is a type of prophecy.

Jesus told me on January 17, 2015 that the next president would be a Christian and restore it doing what is right. He would bless this country and start turning country around back to Him. God is still in control.

Seven (7) is God's number of perfection. The blood moons are signs from God. I heard another prophet say Donald Trump took office at 70 years, 7 months and 7 days. Trump was born in 1946 during a blood moon, 700 days before Israel became a nation. At 1/2 of his term we had a blood moon over Washington, D.C. This is a clear indication of God's choice. Trump will triumph and build the wall for our protection from evil.

Another time Jesus showed me a vision of a golden crown. From the points of the crown rainbows were building, the rainbows curved and went into the person wearing the crown. He said the storm is over that's why the rainbows. Jesus was destroying the problems this person had endured, probably because of praying for this country, but Jesus said He was destroying this country's problems it has been facing for years also.

Part VI

Visions of Heaven

A. JEWELED HEAVEN

Many years ago, Marilyn Monroe sang a song called Diamonds are a Girl's Best Friend. There are certainly a lot of diamonds and beautiful jewels in Heaven. By the way, Jesus is a girl's best friend and some of the first visions Jesus showed me were about diamonds and jewels and the pearl of great price. He showed me a mantle robe covered with diamonds, then He showed me diamond studded shoes and later shoes made up of one whole diamond for each shoe. Another vision was of a golden diamond studded crown and a diamond engagement ring for His church. Jesus showed me these visions Sunday after Sunday in church. I think He was showing me how much He valued the church by showing me diamonds and jewels that are here in our physical Earth so that I would understand His value of the church.

Jesus showed me a vision of His jeweled bride, the church. She had on a white wedding gown with rows of diamonds down the length of the gown. Then He put a golden crown trimmed in diamonds on her head. From the crown golden ribbons started growing. He showed me this series of visions over a month of Sundays. Then on the golden ribbons were diamonds studded in a row. Every week the ribbons got longer. Then all the ribbons became long enough to touch each one of the countries and continents of the world. The church is made up of all people of the world, this is His bride. Another Sunday, the bride had on a cathedral veil trimmed in diamonds and pearls representing the beauty of the bride and the events she had overcome. All of these visions lead me to believe Jesus is coming for His bride soon.

Once in intercessory prayer, Jesus showed me a pair of jeweled epaulets with gold tassels all around the epaulettes and big diamond stars on top. Jesus said we are His commanders praying five-star generals bringing in the many souls for Him, away from the enemy.

Another jeweled vision Jesus showed me was of the water in Heaven called the River of Life. The water is absolutely clear and you can see all the way to the bottom. This vision was of the water that flowed from the throne of God. The sand at the bottom was made up of small pave or chipped up diamonds. In the sand were precious jewels such as sapphires, emeralds, rubies, amethysts, etc. This water is sweet, you can drink it, and also swim in it for joy. It is also healing.

Another vision Jesus showed me was of a mansion. The mansion was made up of huge diamond crowns joined together, even the fence around the mansion was a circlet of diamonds that sur- rounded the whole yard. He is making mansions for all of us. In this mansion, in one room the walls were translucent and filled with the light of Jesus. The bottom of the walls was decorated in a jeweled rose pattern made up of rubies, emeralds, gold and diamonds. It was beautiful.

I also saw a vision of my departed family eating together at a cut crystal dining table, another big diamond. They were sitting on French chairs covered in diamonds. The family was eating and laughing together, enjoying themselves thoroughly. The food was apparently very good and the surroundings were beautiful. It seems the family still celebrates occasions together such as Christmas and Easter as they did on earth.

B. FLORAL VISIONS OF HEAVEN

Jesus showed a vision of a garden gazebo in Heaven. There were flowering trees, blooming flowers, and blooming bushes with a giant domed gazebo and in front of the gazebo were benches to sit on in the floral setting. This was beautiful and another painting was done of this. Jesus seems to love flowers as much or more than me. I received these visions every Sunday. He was showing me pretty pictures to paint and giving me more information about Heaven.

Jesus showed a vision of a mantle made up of beautiful spring flowers such as lilies, peonies, daffodils, hyacinths. It was a lovely mantel and permanent, the flowers didn't fade away. On Valentine's Day another vision of a floral mantle was of open, huge cabbage roses, which covered the whole mantle. Jesus does seem to love flowers as much as me. One day while praying He called me His blood rose. He knows that the rose is my favorite flower and He knows how precious His blood is to me.

C. MANSIONS AND MAJESTIC LOCATIONS

Jesus gave me this information in speech form with visions to offset the information so I would understand better, in prayer time at home. I have a prayer room where I meet Him.

In heaven all homes or mansions are diverse. Some people will live on house boats or large yachts who love the water. Others will live in magnificent log homes in the woods or forests. Others will live in houses that have in their architecture bridges across streams or over small waterfalls. Some homes will be in huge flower gardens. Even flowers can be jeweled in Heaven. We can exchange homes sites for a vacation time with each other.

Weather in Heaven is beautiful at all times to all people. Some people like snow, some sunny, some rain, some very dry desert like! Because people enjoy different weather there is different parts of Heaven. Our mansions are located in the weather we like most.

There are many majestic scenes like here on earth. There are mountain views, prairie or plains, or ocean or desert or woods and forests with streams and waterfalls or jungle. God lets you go visit all majestic scenes and has set up your home in Heaven at your favorite majestic scene. He knows and you your favorite already.

There are all kinds of animals in Heaven and in Heaven no animal is harmful. Our departed pets are waiting for us in heaven.

We can travel throughout the Universe, all we have to do is think it and it becomes real, we are there. Translation I would love to be able to take pictures to paint of different areas of the Universe. Heaven will always be our home base though. Maybe we can take a vacation to visit a floating city in space.

The Lord just showed me recently, we can have vacation homes or cottages. Mine would be at a cottage on the beach.

PREVIEWS OF COMING ATTRACTIONS IN HEAVEN
D. SCHOOLS OF LEARNING IN HEAVEN

There is continual learning in Heaven. You will never be bored. Your IQ increases in Heaven because of deep intimacy with Jesus. Jesus told me all of this information when I was in prayer meditation with Him. He does that if I come to Him and sit in quietness with no distractions. I wait for Him. Some of the different experiences one could have are discussed below:

1. One of my favorite learning situations would be painting with the old art masters like Michelangelo or Leonardo Da Vinci, Rembrandt or Vermeer. How wonderful to be able to learn from the old masters. We can paint with rare jewels in colors we don't have on earth. We would also paint with precious metals as well as regular paint. I can't wait.

2. We could sculpt with amazing materials or do mosaics with jewels instead of glass or stone.

3. School of interior design. We could learn how to help Jesus design mansions. Jesus could explain likes and dislikes to a person and interior designers could help design beautiful, satisfying homes and furnishings.

4. School of transmigration of all people on earth after the flood. Where did Noah's sons go to, what peoples were located where and how. Watching a movie presentation of this would be very interesting. Breaking up of Pangea into the continents also.

5. Being able to see and investigate all parts of the Universe. To be able to see all planets and their moons up close in every solar system, in every galaxy throughout all the Universe. This will be better than seeing some of the Universe through the Hubble telescope views. Jesus has told me the universe has seven sections joined together like a flower with seven petals and a big center of the flower.

6. I would love to see what our planet looked like when Eden was here and where Eden was. I would love to see the pre- flood world especially the dinosaurs. I would love to see Noah's ark, how it was built, where it landed after the flood. Love to see a movie of Jesus' life and his death, burial and resurrection.

7. School of Dance. After being a dance instructor when I was young, this appeals to me a lot. You could learn how to dance in worship to Jesus. Many nations here on Earth have a national dance or dances that represent a certain area. To be able to have the energy and time to learn all the dances would be wonderful. You could dance individually or in groups or teach others to dance. Oh, what fun!

I have listed only a few that appeal to me. I loved art, dance, singing, history, geography and astronomy. Everyone will be able to learn what appeals to them. We will never be bored in Heaven. There are many more schools such as music, writing music, singing, playing musical instruments. There is continual harmonic music in Heaven even from plants.

All problems solved on earth. Since we still have human population on the earth schools of architecture to help them. Schools of weather control. School of engineering. School of design for flying transportation cars, or other means of travel, high speed planes, trains. School of archeology. Schools of economic development so we will have no poverty or starving people on earth. School of robotics to help deep space exploration and settlement on other planets. No extension of evil throughout universe. Gardeners to make beautiful parks that are Eden like on Earth. Agriculture to grow food on other planets.

People on Earth will see and understand the beauty of God and Jesus and Holy Spirit and Heaven and will want to be in Heaven for eternity when their earthly bodies pass. There will be peace and love and unity throughout the Earth as well as in Heaven. My God shall supply all of my needs according to His riches in glory. This will be passed to other planets explored by the people of Earth. They (the people) will still be made in the image of God and good will be brought to the universe as God wills. God will reign over the whole universe and it will be full of His goodness, unity and love. God wants evil to end here not go to in the millennial kingdom on earth, Jesus teaches people of earth how to govern earth correctly.

E. HEAVEN FREE OF DISEASE, ILLNESS AND DEATH

I was told on May 8, 2014 by Jesus about the subject of decaying or aging body while living on earth. I was told while in prayer at home in my prayer room where I try to meet Jesus Monday through Friday like God met Adam every day in Eden until he sinned. We get older or we decay more because of sin on the Earth. Darling, if I am a perfect Jesus and you depend on my perfection and the forgiveness of your sin here and now on Earth, do you have to decay (age) since your sin is taken care of? Do you have to wait for a transformed body after you die or are raptured out of the Earth? Believe that I have transformed your body and it will not decay and your body will work perfect till I call you home. God Jesus still heals perfectly, it is god's will.

I've noticed in my lifetime that Christian intimacy with Jesus seems to keep them, Christians a lot younger looking. Those people that are worldly seem to age quickly and die faster. Even if we are here on Earth physically we are becoming more beautiful in the spirit.

After reading or hearing many accounts of people who have visited Heaven say, when we get to Heaven we have our physical appearance changed. We become youthful again our original hair color, original teeth, no wrinkled skin, and youthful body shape. We will be about the same age as Jesus appears to be. Eternal beauty! Jesus told me in intimacy with Him that the less you sin here on Earth, the less you age. But because of Jesus we are without sin now and can meet with the true one God. Since there will be no disease or physical handicaps in Heaven, you will be free of things like walkers or wheelchairs.

PEOPLE WATCH LOVED ONES FROM HEAVEN

Once while praying Jesus told me my grandmother Lilly was concerned about my mother. Lilly had passed away when my mother was twelve, but apparently still watched over her child from Heaven. I started to pray for Mother, bringing her good Christian books to read and talking to her about what the books said.

About 10 years later while praying again, Jesus said Lilly, my grandmother thanked me. After telling my mother about this, she cried because she realized her mother was still looking out for her even though she was in Heaven and mother was on Earth.

F. In Heaven Jesus will have all aborted babies and babies which have died before becoming mature in their mother's womb in Heaven. These babies will be cared for by their guardian angels and other angels and motherly types which were raptured to Heaven. Jesus will have their baby bodies put back together and made whole and then the babies will be attended and schooled until reaching maturity. There is a special place in Heaven for this. Vision of Jesus putting together a baby. Jesus kisses baby to life, baby smiles to Jesus.

G. Rewards in Heaven

The procedure in order to hear from God is as follows: this is my procedure.

First, go to a prayer area where you will be free from all distractions, a quiet place so the world will not filter in.

Second, I read scripture and say prayers as the Lord's prayer and I ask forgiveness of my sins.

Third, I thank God for taking my body and making it a living sacrifice to Him because of Jesus' sacrifice on the cross.

Fourth, I start praising God for knowing me, this one small person in His entire Universe. It astounds me that He wants to know me.

Fifth, then I go into a spiritual ecstasy trance where I am caught up in the spiritual world and God tells me information about the future, about Heaven, and anything He wants to tell me. I love this experience there is nothing on this Earth that can touch it. This is the most intimate time in the presence with the Lord.

Jesus shows me visions of Him putting on crowns on people constantly. I'm told He is coming back soon with His rewards. You can receive more than one crown because they interlock.

There are five crowns

1. Crown of glory and honor

1 Peter 5:4

"And when the chief Shepherd shall appear, ye shall receive a crown of glory that fadeth not away."

Isaiah 62:3
"Thou shall also be a crown of glory in the hand of the Lord, and a royal diadem in the hand of thy God."

2. Crown of rejoicing

1 Thessalonians 2:19
"For what is our hope or joy, or crown of rejoicing? Are not even ye in the presence of our Lord Jesus Christ at His coming?"

3. Crown of Righteousness

2 Timothy 4:8
"Henceforth there is laid up for me a crown of righteousness, which the Lord, the righteous judge, shall give me at that day: and not to me only, but unto all them also that love His appearing."

4. Crown of life

Revelation 2:10
"Fear none of those things which thou shalt suffer: behold, the devil shall cast some of you into prison, that ye may be tried, and ye shall have tribulation ten days: be thou faithful unto death, and I will give thee a crown of life."

5. Martyr's crown (Sufferer's Crown)

I also call this the martyrs crown or sufferer's crown. Many Christians have undergone persecutions from the enemy and many Christians are being killed for their beliefs in Christ, but it will all be worth it. Heaven is so very magnificent for all eternity and no hate or persecution is there.

We will return these crowns to Jesus because we realize He was the One who helped us receive them.

Part VII

Other Visions From Jesus

In this section we will be talking about the Rapture visions and about the visions when the church returns with Jesus to rule and reign with Him for a thousand years and significant other visions from Jesus.

RAPTURE VISIONS

1. Jesus showed me a picture of the Rapture. A big Jesus was standing in the clouds over the Earth. The departed were pictured as golden dots and the present living as pink dots. They are all passing through His body and He is taking them to His Father in Heaven. Jesus is smiling and happy to see so many people going home with Him. The Holy Spirit pictured as a dove is with Him also because the Holy Spirit played a part in each person's life that was raptured. This was painted.

2. Another rapture vision was of Jesus and a person standing in front of a dark wall in a very dark sinful world. Jesus finds the door and opens it to a world filled with light on the other side. He invites the person through the door with Him to the bright side. This reminds me of the rapture.

3. In intercession I saw a vision of a golden chariot driven by an angel. The angel stopped the golden chariot opened the side door and invited me or you and me to come for the ride of our lives to Heaven. This also reminds me of the rapture.

4. Jesus is coming in the clouds. He is dressed in clouds. He has a golden dove on His chest representing the Holy Spirit and a golden cross in one hand which represents His sacrifice for us. On His head is a golden crown after all He is King of

Kings. He also has golden light rays going through His body and around Him. This became a painting also. Jesus tells me He is coming again soon, be prepared.

JANUARY 30, 2019

Vision while praying of the Wedding Scene. God the Father is holding the Bible and marrying Christ Jesus to His bride. God the father is in the middle of the vision. Jesus is on the right side and Holy Spirit is behind Him. Holy Spirit is the best man and the ring bearer. He also has millions of crowns stacked up beside Him. On the left side are the church, millions of people, Jesus, God the Father and Holy Spirit pleased with the souls saved, that will be with them forever after the marriage they will go in to the wedding feast to celebrate that indescribable love. Jesus is coming soon.

FEBRUARY 3, 2019

Passing a church while on the way in a car to the church my husband and I were attending. I wanted to know what denomination or brand it was. There was no sign in front of the church to give this information. God said soon it will not matter what brand you are-Presbyterian, Baptist, Pentecostal, Methodist or Catholic, because all the churches will be Heavenly and filled with the Holy Fire of God, the greatest revival this country has ever known. The revival will stop all contrived, manmade differences and become God made, Heavenly. This will sweep around the world.

One day while praying, I apologized to the Holy Spirit for talking with and practicing the presence of Jesus. Holy Spirit said 3 in 1 and 1 in 3. I was talking to God the Father, Jesus and the Holy Spirit at the same time without realizing it.

Crown of thorns with 2 white lilies interwoven, represents purity brings with it persecution in this world.

I asked Jesus to keep me humble before Him. He showed me a vision of His feet and I was kissing His feet like the girl in the Bible who was washing His feet with her tears and cleansing with her hair. She did this before His crucifixion.

Then Jesus said, "Would you give your life to me, I gave mine to you. There are many ways to give your life to me, walk as a shining light in this dark world, to show life, not just dying and death. I (Jesus) bring peace, joy, grace and love. You love that love that love lights you from within to show the world what happens when someone gives all of themselves to me, they become beau- tiful in me."

Rev. 22:4

"And they shall see His face, and His name shall be in their fore-heads." Vision of Jesus' hand with holes in it stamping my fore- head. I am strongest with His stamp for eternity, I belong to Jesus.

If a person is killed by another person at 59 it is declared murder.

If a person is killed by another person at 39 it is declared murder.

If a person is killed by another person at 19 it is declared murder.

If a helpless child is killed by another person and the child is 9, it is declared murder.

If a helpless baby in the womb is killed at 9 months or less, it is still murder.

God says we have no right to murder at any stage of being. Good thing our Mothers did not legally murder us because of inconveniency to her. There would be no people to populate the Earth. God brings life not death.

I had a vision of Jesus hugging me and you mightily. I love you so much I died for you, I want you to die to all discouragement, all stops, and problems of the past. Trust me to bring about the revival in your country and around the world, and answer your prayers, for the last great revival or ingathering before the Rapture. I waited so long in order to save more people since the world's population is expanding.

I can't believe how much God loves you and me, He talks to each of us, He knows who each person is in His Kingdom. When you consider how big this Universe is and that it is ever expanding, how much detail there is, how complicated all of it is, yet God still knows each of us personally and demonstrates His love for us. He helps us and answers our prayers with all of our problems.

VISIONS OF THE RETURN FROM HEAVEN

1. Jesus returns with His church. He is riding a white horse. He has on a red robe. All the church are riding white horses, they are in white robes. They are returning to the Earth on a ramp made of clouds. There are angels blowing trumpets announcing the return. There are seven stars in the Heavens representing the seven church ages. Jesus has interlocking golden crowns; His face is lit up and the Sword of the Spirit extends from His mouth. He is King of Kings and Lord of Lords. We are returning to set up His millennial Kingdom on Earth for a thousand years with Satan bound during this time. Satan will not be on Earth to tempt during this time. Jesus will teach the people on Earth what is the perfect will of God and rule with a rod of iron. This became a painting.

2. Jesus showed me this vision a little later. I saw the end of His army going toward Earth from the cloud ramp. Some of the army were splitting off going toward North and South America, others were going to the Far East as Russia, China, Japan, Australia and Indian. Others were going toward Europe and the Middle East. Jesus was trying to show me His Millennial Kingdom would include all the people of the Earth that had made it through the tribulation period.

One of my earliest paintings was of Mary and the baby Jesus. Mary is sitting in a pasture with the mountains of Israel behind her. On her lap is the baby Jesus. He is about two years of age. He is holding a yellow butterfly on His left hand and a yellow bird on His right hand. Mary is holding a rose and she is crowned with a wreath of spring flowers. They are enjoying God's creation. Jesus is holding examples of the insect and animal kingdom and Mary is holding an example of plant life. This was inspired by a closed vision and still one of my favorite paintings.

Vision of Jesus on the cross. Its title is By His Stripes We are Healed. This became a painting. Stripes and wounds are lighted up all over His body and into the atmosphere around Him. In these stripes are located the names of all the diseases we face. Thirty-nine stripes, thirty-nine major diseases even unto death. After all, Jesus overcame death. This became one of my favorite paintings. You can see the pain in His eyes and face but He was willing to do this for us, so we could be free. Thank you, Jesus.

Vision and painting of Mary Magdalene meeting Jesus after His burial and resurrection. Mary Magdalene is crying and reaching out to touch Jesus but He is telling her not to touch Him yet because he has to go to the Father first. There are lines of anointing coming from Jesus going out to touch Mary Magdalene.

Most of the time when I receive visions of Jesus, His face is blotted out by huge rays of light like a sun superimposed over His face but I recognize Him by the love He brings with Him. One time I saw Jesus' face with the Holy Dove imprinted on top. They work, in our lives hand in hand to bring what we need.

One-time Jesus showed me a vision of Him sitting on a huge golden throne in Heaven, and I was sitting on a small golden throne by His side. We all get to sit beside or with Him on our thrones when we get to Heaven. Oh glorious day!

Vision of Jesus holding my hand and we are skipping alone. He is leading me into His joy and peace especially when I am going through an earthly trial. Another thing I have noticed when spending time with Jesus the earthly time seems to fly by especially when you are rewarded with His intimacy.

Lately Jesus has been showing me visions of the wedding ring and our crowns we receive in Heaven as rewards. The wedding ring is a big diamond and all the facets of the diamond look like they have a rainbow in them. In the crown all the diamonds have rainbows in the facets. This reminds me of God's throne room pictured with the rainbow. This also may mean the next big revival will be a God revival not just a Jesus or Holy Spirit revival, all will be involved.

Another vision God has shown me is of Jesus at the transfiguration. God the Father was in a cloud with His hands outstretched toward His son, Jesus. His hands surrounding His Son. The first painting I saw of the transfiguration, I was in an art history class looking at slides of various pictures. When I saw this painting, I made a mental commitment to try to paint a scene similar to it. I have tried but nothing can compare to the real thing, the beauty of Jesus. Jesus showed me a vision of a royal banner to sew for the church I attended. The banner has a jeweled crown for God the Father, a jeweled cross for Jesus and a jeweled dove made of pearls. There are lines of colored jewels extending from each panel, these represent the people in the church which have a connected relationship with the Holy Trinity. On the outside of the panels are diamond jewels which represent the intercessors in the church or the guardians of the church. I did manage to complete this banner.

Speaking of jeweled visions, I have seen visions of gold coins falling from Heaven around us and also our paper money in stacks around us. Jesus does truly want our needs met. While at church I have seen actual gold dust on clothing and miracles of teeth being replaced with gold teeth which last forever for the person here on earth.

While praying recently Jesus showed me a little girl's head with a red bow on each side of her head. Sometimes I have to wait to understand what He is trying to tell me. The final understanding of this vision was wonderful to me. The bows are red representing the blood of Jesus. Jesus said one bow was for my mind, I would not get Alzheimer's as did my mother. The other bow was for my daughter who is bipolar and still needs healing. Jesus told me to keep praying for her healing. Is there anything too hard for me?

One day while praying in a local high school we were trying to discern if God wanted a new church started there. I saw a vision of the largest angel I've ever seen. The angel had to be at least thirty feet tall. The large angel was at the ceiling of the High School, the small angels were standing, guarding in the doorways. Good thing to know God loves our teenagers enough to place angels around them and above them to protect them. I also saw angels in each doorway.

Saw a vision of the Holy Spirit depicted as a series of refreshing and cleansing water falls, falling on people that needed to be forgiven and forgiving and calmed and loved and healed. Thank you, Holy Spirit, for your cleansing and redeeming power.

Jesus showed a vision of an anointing going through a tube, it was called a dark tube anointing and hidden. This changed to a light tube anointing. The tube was filled with gold and the anointing was open or clearly understood.

Another vision was of a heart hooked up to two separate olive trees. This represented constant nourishment of anointing.

Part VIII

Miracles Go On To The Next Generation, The Beat Goes On

Once when my son and I were going through the hardest time of our lives his father, my husband had died and we had lost about seven people in the immediate family in a short period of time. Mike went out on the patio and Jesus showed him an actual portal that went up into Heaven. We figured out later this was a calling on his life to serve God. Then Mike and I went to Israel together. Then Mike was healed of multiple sclerosis, cigarette and pot smoking and dyslexia. All of this changed his life so Mike went to Rhema Bible College.

My son was teaching Sunday School one Sunday. He had recently been diagnosed with an uneven heartbeat and the doctor thought my son's heart was damaged. Each child in that Sunday school class came up one by one and placed their hands on Mike's heart and prayed for him. My son, Mike went back to the doctor and his heart was fine no damage. This is teaching children that God, Jesus and the Holy Spirit does heal even today.

Another time the Sunday school class was baptized in the Holy Spirit, half of them received tongues as proof that they had received baptism. This will never be forgotten by those children. Mike feels he has found his destiny, his way to serve the Lord.

My daughter has been a true challenge. She has been diagnosed as a bipolar schizophrenia since she was about 21. God has protected her in two car wrecks and three overdoses of her mediations when she was depressed. She should have died each time but God protected her and still has plans for her life. God told me to still pray for her not to give up.

Vision of a royal robe falling on you from Heaven. In your hand God is placing a golden staff and, on your head, a religious crown like a miter.

This vision is a royal robe falling on Christians from Heaven. In your hand God is placing a golden staff, on your head, a religious crown like a miter.

Jesus says," *I am making you a royal priesthood holy and accept- able in my sight after the order of Melchizedek.*" (Psalm 110:4)

Jesus wants to be sure you get to Heaven and its perfection. Another painting of a vision called "Choose". It was of Jesus pointing to a scene in Heaven with one of His arms and with the other arm pointing to a planet that looked like a burning hell. Please dear people "*choose*" correctly. Come soon Lord Jesus. See you in Paradise!

Part IX

Invitations

Dear children Jesus loves you and longs for you to be with Him and the Holy Trinity throughout all eternity. Please pray acceptance for Jesus to come into your life and forgive you of your sins and live with Him always. This will give you great peace and you will feel His love and grace and wonder how you ever lived without Jesus.

Jesus has also made a way for you to be baptized in the Holy Spirit. The Holy Spirit makes a way for deeper intimacy with Jesus, God the Father and the Holy Spirit. Ask the Holy Spirit to come into your life and give you the gift of tongues and the other gifts listed in I Corinthians 12:7-11. The Holy Spirit will give you the gifts you desire most or the gifts He knows you will need in your life. The gift of tongues is proof to show you the Holy Spirit did this for you.

God wants to know you and fellowship with you always. God made this Universe, this galaxy, this solar system and this perfectly placed planet and then all of mankind. He knows you and wants to have fellowship with you. He knows of everything you will need and the answers to all your problems. God is truly love. Give Him a chance. Love him back, have a relationship with him.

Mary and Baby Jesus.

By his stripes I am healed.

Choose Heaven or Hell.

Christ Appearing.

The Rapture

After the Storm

Crown of Thorns

Church Bride Looking At His Wounds

The Return

THE END

Words *of* Wisdom

Book 2

When I look back at the last 4 years, since 2021, I am amazed how God loved me enough to help me and my family withstand such turbulent times.

God did this by giving me many prophecies to relieve stress and worry about what we, my family, were encountering every day. It almost seemed like Satan and his plans for this country were getting more obvious every day with continual bad news. But God the Father, Jesus, and the Holy Spirit are much more powerful than Satan, and they rescued this country, no matter how foolish mankind has been by following the plans of Satan.

Here are some of the words of wisdom God gave to me during these years in sequential order.

Dec. 19, 2021

Because you know and love Jesus, your walk in Heavenly paradise here on Earth even as the world and your country go through hellish events every day.

I asked God that His heavenly love be in every room in my house and all the people in this house. I also asked God that His presence of love will be on us when we go out into the world, and this love would pass over everyone we come in contact with.

Jan. 12, 2021

Jesus has been telling me I am coming again soon every day for at least 2 weeks. Jesus is not taking His people out via the Rapture, but He is coming to Earth to step on and out of the evil that the enemy has snuck into America.

The false election, and Trump's having no one to fight for him but the 79 million Christian supporters, not government elected officials.

Jesus showed me a picture of His big foot coming down to the United States and starting to stomp out corruption, and Jesus keeps on stomping on evil and corruption until it is wiped out. Thank you, Jesus.

Nov. 15, 2021

I received a vision of Jesus's back after 39 lashes with streams of blood going down His back. Then a picture of me hugging His back with my face in the blood stream, loving on Him and His sacrifice.

Nov. 27, 2021

I wanted to know why Jesus kept warning me that He is coming back soon and wanted me and my family ready to go.

He said, if I don't think you are worthy, why would I keep talking to you? Why would I keep reminding you? If I did not care, you would not hear from me, and remind you that you will be in my loving embrace forever soon.

Vision of a crown going on my head again. You made it worthy of me dying on a cross. You alone were worth it, and I have many others who made it worth me dying on a cross for them. Jesus is the only God who was willing to die for mankind.

Feb. 6, 2022

Vision: I saw a vision of a peacock with tail Feathers spread out like a fan. It's absolutely beautiful. The peacock here is a symbol of a human being who has given their life to Jesus and the Holy Spirit. With Jesus and the Holy Spirit in us we become more beautiful every day in every way, hence our tail feathers are beautiful all the time.

Feb. 7, 2022

Vision: A giant bib is being placed over my head. The bib covers my front and sides and even my back. Jesus said He is putting this on me to protect me from the worldly slop and garbage being constantly thrown at me though the media, bad situations, and witches and warlocks trying to place curses on me. Jesus said the slop and garbage bounces off of me back to where it came from.

Again if you follow Jesus you will have persecution in your life, don't be troubled, I Jesus am your sword and shield.

Jan. 23, 2022

Reading about the New Heavens and New Earth. People with heavenly bodies will ve in Heaven just above the Earth. People with fleshly bodies will be on Earth and because Satan and all his minions have been obliterated, all the fleshly people on Earth are not tempted to sin. This will be just like the Garden of Eden before Satan showed up to tempt Adam and Eve.

God tells me that He will let mankind go into the rest of the universe to settle other planets, and the Heavenly population will help them. God had to settle the sin issue here on Earth before He would let the rest of the universe be settled, so all the universe could truly be a garden of Eden.

Jan. 30, 2022 - Kings and Priests of Melchisadec

Vision of a mantle of red velvet with ermine on the inside, this mantle reaches all the way down to the floor. Also, a crown of gold with red jewels to form a cross in the center.

A golden scepter in the shape of a cross in your right hand is to show you are a ruler.

White robe underneath the mantle. You are seated on a golden throne with a red cushion on the seat. The red cushion represents the blood of Christ.

Jan. 31, 2022 - Kings & Priests of Melchisadec

There are golden slippers with rubies evenly spaced around them.

Jesus is the King and High Priest of the Order of Melchisadec, and He tells me that because we are His followers, we are also Kings and Priests of Melchisadec also.

Feb. 1, 2022

The lily is a sign of the righteousness of Jesus's purity.

I saw a vision of a white lily kissing me on my cheek, then clapping its petals in applause because I was a follower of Jesus, who is purity and love.

Feb. 2, 2022

God (Holy Spirit) can give words of peace to turn situations around.

When staying at my mother and Father-in-Law's house, my Father-in-Law came into the house accusing me of some violation against him. The Holy Spirit opened my mouth, and His words of wisdom.

Feb. 2, 2022

Came out, reprieving me from my stepfather's accusations and anger. Too bad all our diplomats, ambassadors, and politicians are not baptized in the Holy Spirit. This would definitely create a more loving and kind world.

Feb. 3, 2022

Vision: Jesus is standing at the entrance to Heaven and turning down a rich man's entrance.

Money can't buy your way into Heaven. Many rich feel like they can have anything they want, after all, they have access to everything and are higher than all of the little people beneath them and they should have everything and more than the little people will ever have. This does not work in getting into Heaven.

Jesus loves the humble servant, especially the ones who love Him.

It is harder for a rich man to get into Heaven than for a camel to go through the eye of a needle. Mark 10:24 and 25.

Vision: Jesus puts a crown on my head and hugs me to Him. Thank you, Jesus, for always reassuring me, for loving me, and giving me your peace.

Feb. 4, 2022

Vision: I have seen this vision so many times, flowers with words printed on them.

Jesus is the word; Jesus writes His words on the flowers. We, the people, are the flowers in His garden. His words are written on us and in us.

Vision #2 I see dirty crowns with dirty crystals hanging from them.

Many prophetic men like to talk and write about bad news or bad things happening on Earth. They should be talking and writing about the good things happening in Heaven, and that will also be happening on Earth. They also should be praying for good things to happen on this Earth always.

Feb. 5, 2022

I feel like a fish out of water in this society, but I will be completely comfortable in Heaven, and when we all are near Heaven, many will feel like fish out of water, but I will feel completely at home. Thank you, Jesus.

Feb. 5, 2022

The light coming through leaves, twigs, branches, or on the trees are repeatedly 3 dots representing Father, Son, & Holy Spirit.

I see the Father on one side, the Son on the other side, Holy Spirit at the bottom.

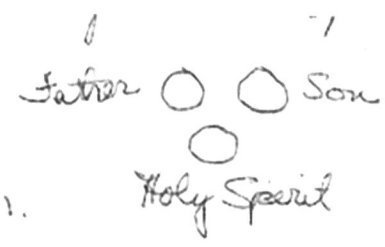

The Father and Son up on top, they are in Heaven. The Holy Spirit is at the bottom representing Earth. The Holy Spirit comforts, loves, teaches, gives spiritual gifts and wisdom. Holy Spirit knows what everyone is thinking and if you are a person who will rely on Him, He will give you what Jesus and the Father want you to have, your destiny, prosperity, health, and wisdom. Sometimes to see four circles that represent the cross.

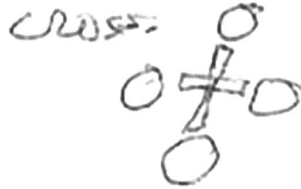

Not my will but they will be done, Jesus told us God the Father 3 times what the Father wanted, so Jesus went to the crucifixion for us so we could be forgiven of our sins. When Jesus says to me something I don't want to do particularly, I say not my will but thy will be done.

When you follow Jesus, you will have persecution as He did.

Feb. 6, 2022

Vision: I saw a vision of a peacock with tail feathers spread out like a fan. It's absolutely beautiful. The peacock here is a symbol of a human being who has given their life to Jesus and the Holy Spirit. With Jesus and the Holy Spirit in us we become more beautiful every day in every way, hence our tail feathers are beautiful all the time.

Feb. 7, 2022

Vision: A giant bib is being placed over my head. The bib covers my front and sides and even my back. Jesus said He is putting this on me to protect me from the worldly slop and garbage being constantly thrown at me though the media, bad situations, and witches and warlocks trying to place curses on me. Jesus said the slop and garbage bounces off of me back to where it came from.

Again if you follow Jesus you will have persecution in your life, don't be troubled, I Jesus am your sword and shield.

Feb. 8, 2022

Learn to turn the other cheek.

I have withstood persecution from witches and warlocks on my car. The first time a warlock opened the back of his truck, the tailgate and scraped the entire front of my car, a SUV, so that my husband had to put new headlights in front and patch the front dent along the entire front of my car, then repaint everything. I turned the other cheek #1.

The second time the same warlock scratched or keyed a long line along the side of the fresh paint job, to show me he was the one who dented my car. I turned the other cheek #2.

The third time my husband was driving my car at 7 o'clock in the morning and a deer buck who was huge purposely attacked the car. My husband did not run into the deer buck, the buck intentionally ran into him (a curse from warlocks).

The police officer that reported the accident said he had never seen such a big buck. The buck was very injured so the policeman shot the buck to put it out of misery. The damage to the car was unbelievable and expensive to fix, but it was done and God prepared a way to have the most of the expense paid so I didn't have to. I have turned the other cheek again #3.

Feb. 9, 2022

Witches and warlocks have harassed me for at least 15 years.

They have tried to intimidate me but Jesus is the stronger one and on my side. How do they know where you are? Satan tells them.

They, witches or warlocks, have met me in art stores, drug stores, grocery stores, parking lots, and even tried to run me off of the highway when I was driving my car. My husband has approached these people and they fled because they knew my husband would protect me. They have tried to stop God's good, but they can't.

I learned to surround our property with the blood of Jesus so they can't come on our property, but that did not work either. I ask Jesus every night in prayer to surround our property, our vehicles, our house and shed and especially us the people with His blood. Witches and warlocks do not like the blood of Jesus. It amazes me that they want to serve Satan and be in hell forever. I now pray that Jesus will change their minds and save them. Jesus has saved many evil people and loves changing their minds and saving them.

Feb. 11, 2022

Why are people so down and discouraged now? Have I God changed? Is anything too hard for me? I God am the giver of all good things. I have not changed. Believe in a good God who gives good things and you will see in your life good and good things. Believe in a good God and I God will come in as good in your churches and in your lives and in your land and it will become worldwide. In fact it is worldwide but not yet recognized.

Feb. 14, 2022

Today we on Earth celebrate Valentine's Day by giving out gifts of hearts and candy. Jesus gave us the best Valentine's Day present by giving us His heart and the delicious taste of His sacrifice so we could experience His love and Heaven forever, the very gift of gifts of all time.

Feb. 15, 2022

Love is forever! God's love never changes. He loves us despite our unloveliness.

Feb. 15, 2022

God's love is always consistent. He does not change. If I mess up or goof up, He still loves me until I straighten up. Yeh God!

Feb. 16, 2022

When I watch the fowls of the air, I am amazed at their capabilities and how many kinds there are. They go from the size of an ostrich down to the size of a hummingbird. They also go to artic homes. In my location, different birds are prevalent in different seasons. It is a joy to see ducks and geese fly over in the fall going to a warmer location.

Birds here build nests, lay eggs and then keep them warm. When the eggs hatch, the mother and father feed them and teach them everything they need to know. When I compare birds with humans, I see some similarities. Most human parents try to teach their children everything they will need to know and support them until they are capable of supporting themselves. But humans often think they know better than God how to do everything, but they should remember God is our original parent.

Feb. 16, 2022

We were made in His likeness and image, but Satan fooled us and continues to do so. So God the Father had to send His perfect Son to save us from sin, so we could go to Heaven, our final destination. God also gave us a book of instruction the Bible to help us learn and live correctly because He loves us. I wish we always loved Him as well as He loves us. We can also pray to the Holy Spirit and He will tell us what or how to do correctly.

Feb. 21, 2022 Presidents' Day

After watching a T.V. program about George Washington and Abraham Lincoln you realize what magnificent things they did for this country. They each had a strong relationship with God and did as God advised them. I wish more presidents were like these 2 presidents.

What these 2 presidents did ought to be taught to students in all our classrooms, so they could understand men of honor who served and obeyed the Lord God and then how God blessed them.

George Washington wrote a government of the people, by the people, for the people and every man created equal. George Washington designed Washington D.C. God led Washington to fight for this country against the British and Washington won most of the battles.

When in the 5th grade, I got to see one of George Washington's uniforms with bullet holes in it, but God did not allow George Washington to be shot. Lincoln freed all the slaves in this country and said all men are free and equal.

Feb. 24, 2022 Russia attacked Ukraine today.
The Ukrainians are trying to get to Poland or out in the country, away from their cities, which are being destroyed by Russia.

Feb. 28
Vision: Saw a golden ring with a golden butterfly on top of the ring. The butterfly was filled with diamonds.

In the worm stage – crawling in the world knowledge.
In the cocoon stage – being taught of Christ.
In the butterfly stage – baptized in the freedom of the Holy Spirit.

March 2, 2022 Ash Wednesday

In the Bible it says you can live to 70 and 80 if you are strong. I am now 84 and I wonder how I am still here. Because I walk in Jesus, Jesus walks in me. Jesus gives you strength in mind, body, and soul. I am walking in His strength, not my strength.

March 3, 2022

I am coming again, child, I have not forgotten my promise. I know you and others have been waiting for a long time, but my timing is perfect as you will see.

Vision: You saw a lace-like crown of gold with beautiful gemstones called amethysts.

Don't give up on me. I know life on Earth is getting difficult but I will rescue my own before the 7 years of tribulation truly begin, but we are close. Trust me, I will not leave you or forsake you because I love you.

Some prophets are always talking bad news and lately we have definitely had a lof of bad news, especially about Russia making war on Ukraine. Don't advertise what Satan is doing.

March 4, 2022 – Friday

Trust God, Jesus and the Holy Spirit. They are powerful, but kind and loving also. Trust God for revival to this nation and other nations, especially for the people who don't know Him and need Him.

March 5, 2022

Jesus is the son of man as well as the Son of God. God loved us, mankind, whom He had made so much He God was willing to ask His Son to come to Earth to be the son of man even if He Jesus was the Son of God. Then Jesus obeying His Father came to Earth to save mankind of his sin. This love always astounds me.

March 6, 2022

Vision: Heels with small interwoven turquoise stones on them. Jesus explained while here on Earth you can have a small bit of a Heavenly walk, not as complete as your Heavenly walk with diamonds on your shoes.

Those of you who know Jesus get to see and understand what Heaven will be like, which sustains you until you get into the real Heaven.

March 6, 2022

I can't wait, no more cleaning, cooking, chores, doctors, or dentists. You stay young and are never ill, I sure hope I will not be selected for kitchen duties or housekeeping duties. Heaven needs chefs and cleaning people.

Vision: Different shoe patterns are as symbols of a more or less Heavenly walk.

March 7, 2022

If you really want to help your nation, repent of all the sins of your nation. Even though you had nothing to do with a lot of these sins, repent to God for all the sins you can think of. God wants a repentant spirit and confession of all sin and your repentant prayer may be able to help your nation or country. You can also repent to God for other nations or countries that are doing wrong.

We would also repent for so many turning away from God or thinking He does not exist anymore. We could repent for killing or aborting so many babies. We could repent for how many times His God's name is taken in vain or cussed with His name. When this country gets in trouble, we are going to want God's help immediately.

March 7, 2022

If we repented of the sins of our nation, maybe we wouldn't get plaques like Cov-19 or foul weather like hurricanes and tornadoes. Repentance can lead to revival.

We could repent for the sins of Russia and China for what they have done to their people and other people around the world.

March 8, 2022
Dream: Often when I pray for my husband or others, especially for the protection of Jesus. When I get through praying Jesus will tell me in my spirit, Done Daughter so loudly, I almost feel His presence there. When Jesus says Done Daughter, I know I don't have to worry about the situation I was praying about and I can relax and know Jesus is taking care of everything.
This is very encouraging and you can do this too.

March 9, 2022
Dream: Reagan was an actor and Trump a businessman, but both were not career politicians, but both were excellent presidents.

March 10, 2022

I wish T.V. did not advertise sickness and disease. It's a wonder people live as well as they do, instead of winding up with all of the advertised diseases. It's almost as if they want you to have these diseases in order to test their medications.

Won't you try a little cancer, or COPD or diabetes or other diseases? Take only the medicines your doctor prescribes. Jesus is your best medicine also.

March 11, 2022
Found our today cigarettes are over $60.00 a carton, made me realize sin is expensive. 3 cartons of cigarettes are $180.00 dollars. If you are addicted to drugs, alcohol, etc. it is expensive. Hence sin is expensive. Satan beats people down with addictions, then you have to pay Satan to kill you.

March 14, 2022
Sin really bothers me and bothers most Christians. Christians have read the Bible

March 14, 2022

And try to live by God's word and laws found in the Bible. It amazes me to see the sin committed every day in my country and elsewhere, all the lying in the media, to see what Russia is doing to the people in Ukraine. Scammers calling my home every day trying to con me out of money.

I have noticed another thing, the world is not a happy place because of all the sin. Because I believe what the Bible says and I know how much Jesus loves us I can stay happy no matter how much sin I see and I know I will go to a happy place called Heaven when I leave this Earth of sin. Also I am amazed at the patience of God, as He deals with this sinful world, but God always tries to bless us and save us because somehow He still loves us, despite the sin.

March 15, 2022

One day all sin will be taken out of the world and we will be able to live in perfection with God the Father, God the Son, and God the Holy Spirit. We will be able to live in an Eden-like environment like Adam and Eve with God until they were fooled by Satan and sinned.

March 15, 2022

How wonderful Jesus came to this Earth and showed us how and made it possible to have no sin. To live in the presence of Jesus is wonderful. Thank you Father God, thank you Jesus, and thank you Holy Spirit. The Holy Spirit helps mold us into the image of Jesus, and what Jesus did.

March 16, 2022

Jesus sent us the Holy Spirit, the Holy Spirit helps us not only to be like Jesus but also to do what Jesus did. The Holy Spirit enters our bodies with His fire and enables us to help others as Jesus did. When the Holy Spirit enters I start shaking in my hands and praising and praying the language of tongues.

I don't know what I am praying but the Holy Spirit does, it is often to help others find answers they need through God, Jesus, and the Holy Spirit.

March 17, 2022 St. Patrick Day

St. Patrick was born in Wales of two Irish parents. He was captured by an Irish slave ship when he was a young boy. He did Compare himself to King David who kept sheep like he did when young. God sent an angel to direct St. Patrick how to escape. He crossed the sea to Wales and walked 23 miles to his home. Then as a young man he went to France to study how to become a missionary. He studied for 15 years. Then St. Patrick went back to Ireland and saved thousands of people. At that time many Irish people worshiped idols and strange gods. St. Patrick built many churches throughout Ireland because many Irish people were saved. He died on March 17th in Northern Ireland hence March 17th is St. Patrick's Day.

March 18, 2022

St. Patrick said he felt the presence of God on top of him, he felt God at the bottom on him, on each side of him and all throughout him. God also told him what to think and say. I'm sure most Christians who are truly devoted to God feel the same things.

April 18, 2022

Told today me and 2 children would be dead by now if we did not believe in Jesus.

May 18, 2022

Went to the doctor then the dentist today with my daughter. As Dr. Campbell the dentist said, it was a Double D Day. But it was also a Triple G Day. God the Father, God the Son, and God the Holy Spirit. It is always a Triple G Day.

When my daughter and I were coming back home, we stopped to fill her tank up with gas. I went inside the store to get a treat, and God gave me a treat. I saw a beautifully, handsome man with white hair, a short sleeve shirt with white and light blue stripes, belt and trousers. His eyes were a deep blue and his face shown with light. He looked directly into my eyes and smiled.

In prayer, God later told me this was my guardian angel whom I had never seen before. What a treat, your guardian angel knows who you are and is always on the job, protecting your from evil.

May 20, 2022

Reminded again to pray against abortion which God considers murder. In the United States we have killed 63 million babies, I wonder if God is going to kill 63 million people in our country. With Covid 19 that may be a real possibility. My state still aborts babies, please stop killing innocent humans. The Supreme Court should never have let this go to a state decision, especially after the Supreme Court decided it was wrong. These aborted babies have a special place in Heaven.

May 21, 2022

When loved ones leave the Earth and go to Heaven, they are greeted by their family members who have gone to Heaven before them and they all celebrate together. Jesus wishes this could happen to all people who pass away, that they would all go to Heaven to be with other loved ones and celebrate, but some go to Hell to be there forever.

In Heaven everyone there operates and believes in the power of God and His kingdom, that's why Heaven is so Heavenly.

God says fear not, for I will never leave thee, be not afraid because I am thy God. God is all knowing and all seeing.

Jan. 2, 2023

Jesus told me Israel is going to have the ability to return rockets launched at them, return to the source from which they came. Jesus told me they were working on this last year. For example Israel has many rockets fired at them every day and Israel has blown those rockets up as best they could. But because so many rockets are fired at them from the South and North and West they can't get all of them.

With this new system, when Israel sees or discovers a rocket coming in or many rockets coming in, Israel will be able to turn around the rockets and send them back home to where they came from. This will discourage rockets being fired at them ever again.

This will be a great system to discourage any country firing missiles on any other country. This could help stopping wars between countries.

March 7, 2023

Even though everything seems to be going crazy and receiving bad news constantly,

March 7, 2023

If you walk with Jesus and the Holy Spirit, your environment or walk seems to be Heavenly paradise no matter what is going on around you on Earth. You feel God's peace and joy and nothing can bring you down from your Heavenly walk in paradise.

March 8, 2023

If you have been Baptized in the Holy Spirit, you carry Holy Spirit around on the inside of you or in your body. This means the Holy Spirit can enable you to talk to Jesus, God the Father, as well as the Holy Spirit. Be conscious of which you take your body to, and what you expose the Holy Spirit to, as example what are you watching on T.V.? What are you saying to other people? Are you blessing them? Would the Holy Spirit like what you are saying? Try to be kind and loving as God is. Ask the Holy Spirit to help you express no anger and no criticism.

March 9, 2023

Many men feel like they can lie and cheat people and the people will never know it. If you are a Christian or someone who loves Jesus, you will be able to discern liars and cheats easily because the Holy Spirit disclose them to Christians. It's like Jesus gives you the ability (His ability) to discern corruption of any type. Corruption makes your spirit uneasy. You can't hide or lie about who or what you are; it is painfully obvious.

A cheat and liar may be able to fool for a while, but Jesus and the Holy Spirit will make it very obvious. Politicians might to remember this and never lie and cheat the American people especially Christians who discern with Jesus and the Holy Spirit. Can you fool God?

March 10, 2023

Don't murder others with the words of your mouth. Your words should uplift and bless others and not hurt them. In the Bible nasty words are considered murderous words. Don't murder with your mouth. God only says good things about you and other people, you do the same.

March 10, 2023

As my mother use to say, if you can't say something nice about someone, don't open your mouth.

Also don't murder others with your mind. Don't think ill of others in your mind. God does not like that. Think good thoughts of others, God certainly does.

After watching a Christian show about what God did to create an environment so man could live and be located where we are and then to create mankind. In other words God created the whole universe around the needs of a created man. It amazes me that God loves us so much, He did this for us. He knew everything we as people would need and provided it for us just like Genesis I says.
I feel like this small little part of creation can talk to the Creator of the Universe and how blessed I feel, for God to bother for me.

March 20, 2023

I feel astounded that I am able to talk to the Creator of the Universe and His only Son Jesus through the power of the Holy Spirit. Why would the Creator of the ever expanding Universe want to talk to one little person He created? Then God reminded me of how He created Adam and Eve and talked with Adam especially every day. God likes to talk with His creation. God made mankind in His image so He could fellowship with them. Then He made His Son Jesus take away our sins so we could be pure enough to talk with our creator and even live in Heaven with them. God's love still astounds me.

March 17, 2023

The computer development is getting to be more and more especially AI or artificial intelligence. I can see how the Anti Christ will be able to discern and know what's going on with the entire world population and make everyone do his will. The Anti Christ will be able to make the world population do what he wants or he will destroy everyone who doesn't obey him.

Thank Heavens, Christians will be in Heaven with Jesus after the Rapture.

The people that have accepted Jesus as their savior are more nearly perfect than any man that walks on the Earth. A man hooked up to a computer which enables him to have an IQ over a thousand is not the most perfect man in the world. Artificial intelligence is just that artificial.

The smartest most perfect man is the man that has accepted Jesus the Son of God as their savior. After all God and Jesus and Holy Spirit made the whole universe, which is still growing. No artificial intelligence can come anywhere near the intelligence of an omniscient God or His Son Jesus or the Holy Spirit.

Artificial intelligence may appeal to certain people to make them feel like they are God, but they will never catch up to God the Father or His Son or the Holy Spirit.

Why would you want man made inferior when you can have God made Superior?

March 23, 2023

While sitting in an art history class when I was in college I saw a painting of a small Jesus. Then God put in my heart to paint pictures of Jesus that were bigger and brighter and showed my love for Him and His love for me and all other people who would acknowledge Jesus as their Savior.

March 24, 2023

When I look outside at all of the trees, branches, & leaves, I see a pattern of Jesus's face repeatedly. These are constant reminders of who created all of those trees, branches, & leaves. Who created planet Earth, who created mankind, and who was willing to die for us so we could be saved and have eternal life and not taste of death.

Mankind could not be sin free, but Jesus could. Thank you, Jesus, for taking all of my sin, so I could go to Heaven and be with you, and the Father, and the Holy Spirit forever. And thank you for sending the

Holy Spirit so I can communicate with you and hear you say Jesus, you love me. You died for me because you love me. I Jesus would have died just for you, one person but because I was willing to die, many people will be saved and be with me forever in my eternal Kingdom.

March 27, 2023

If people who encounter bad, killing weather such as tornadoes, hurricanes, floods, would find it in their hearts and find time to pray to me to bless them with weather that reflects my peace, joy, stillness, etc., life on Earth and in the United States would be better. Children draw close to me, pray for my peace in the weather and atmosphere in your country. I still control all, even the weather and no emphasis on the Green Deal works for mankind, but emphasis on me will. Love God.

March 25, 2023

Jesus kissed me on closed eye lids, then on my forehead and then on my mouth. It became a perfect cross pattern.

It is so wonderful for God, Jesus to show you how much He loves you.

April 11, 2023

When up in the morning, I thought about reading my scripture lesson, but God told me to do something totally different, which surprised me. He told me to turn on the T.V. and I found the program He wanted me to watch. The program was about a very successful lady lawyer who saved the day for a well-known man.

I had been reading scripture in Corinthians and felt like those women were second grade of nature and not to well thought of, and should not be allowed to be in religious activity. God showed me He loves godly, successful women. Jesus certainly loved the women He encountered. I learned that I did not have to be a second grade person just because I am a female.

If it were not for females having male babies, the male would not exist.

Vision: Gold hands in shape of heart, golden rod in center with a spinning ruby heart on the golden rod. The ruby represents the blood of Christ. The hands of gold represent God the Father.

After finishing the 2nd booklet, Satan came during the night and tormented me with back aches and rib aches and I could not go to sleep, but finally got up and took 2 Aleve for night and that worked.

Then I slept soundly until 8:00 o'clock the next morning. Thank you, Jesus. Jesus also told me to write another booklet (the third) about the Holy Spirit. Thank you, Jesus.

March 10, 2024

You came and gave yourself, Jesus, so I could have all of you.

May 14, 2024

Vision of a huge golden crown with a veil or curtain around it, then the veil opens. God reminded me of the veil opening when we get to Heaven

Nov. 17, 2021

The blood sacrifices of Jesus are listed below, sacrifices for us.

1. He sweat blood while praying
2. Whipped on His back, by His stripes we are healed
3. A crown of thorns
4. & 5. His 2 feet nailed to the cross
6. & 7. His 2 hands nailed to the cross
8. Speared in side

Jan. 23, 2022

Reading about the New Heavens and New Earth. People with heavenly bodies will ve in Heaven just above the Earth. People with fleshly bodies will be on Earth and because Satan and all his minions have been obliterated, all the fleshly people on Earth are not tempted to sin. This will be just like the Garden of Eden before Satan showed up to tempt Adam and Eve.

God tells me then He will let mankind go into the rest of the universe to settle other planets and the Heavenly population will help them. God had to settle the sin issue here on Earth before He would let the rest of the universe be settled so all the universe could truly be a garden of Eden.

Jan. 30, 2022 - Kings and Priests of Melchisadec

Vision of a mantle of red velvet with ermine on inside, this mantle reaches all way down to the floor. Also a crown of gold with red jewels to form a cross in the center.

A golden scepter in the shape of a cross is in your right hand is to show you are a ruler.

White robe underneath the mantle. You are seated on a golden throne with a red cushion on the seat. The red cushion represents the blood of Christ.

Jan. 31, 2022 - Kings & Priests of Melchisadec

There are golden slippers with rubies evenly spaced around them.

Jesus is the King and High Priest of the Order of Melchisadec and He tells me because we are His followers, we are Kings and Priests of Melchisadec also.

Feb. 1, 2022

The lilly is a sign of righteousness of Jesus's purity.

I saw a vision of a white lilly kissing me on my cheek, then clapping its petals in applause because I was a follower of Jesus, who is purity and love.

Feb. 4, 2022

Vision. I have seen this version many times, flowers with words printed on them. Jesus is the word, Jesus writes on the flowers His words, We the people are the flowers in His garden, His words are written on us and in us.

Vision #2 I see dirty crowns with dirty crystals hanging from them.

Many prophetic men like to talk and write about bad news, or bad things happening on Earth. They should be talking and writing about the good things happening in Heaven and that will also be happening on Earth. They also should be praying for good things to happen on this Earth always.

Feb. 5, 2012

I feel like a fish out of water in this society, but I will be completely comfortable in Heaven and when we all are near Heaven many will feel like Fish out of water, but I will feel completely at home. Thank you Jesus

Jan. 16, 2025

Since my birthday, May 14, 2024, my husband has truly been tested. On my birthday, he took the trash to the dump, made a right hand turn from the dump to come home. He was on a double lane highway coming home and there was another double lane highway on the other side going toward Port Royal.

All of a sudden this car smashed into him and my Honda SUV. Satan has been trying to destroy this car ever since I purchased it. My husband landed on the outside of the road down a hill and his arm was hurt. God saved him because he could have been killed.

The woman driving the car that smashed into him was talking on a phone, smoking a cigarette, and she said she couldn't see him. Really? He was in a red Honda. Eventually he was operated on his arm and things were beginning to correct or look better.

Lately he has been diagnosed with diverticulitis and has lost at least 18 lbs.

My husband has shown remarkable spiritual growth lately and has been punished by Satan in order to discourage him. But knowing my husband, this will never stop him.

Dec. 31, 2024

Last day of 2024 which was hard to the core thanks to the Democrats.

In 2025 you will thrive especially with Trump and more of God by your side.

Jan. 22, 2025

I told you previously that the world would be entering a cold cycle and I told you it would start in 2025. Do not be alarmed at the weather change. It is cyclic and has gone on this Earth forever. There is no such thing as just global warming.

Jan. 27, 2025

When Trump almost lost his life at the assassination attempt, he gave his life to me & God helped him become president of the United States and I God guarantee you, Trump will be the best president this country has ever had. Trump will be better than any previous president because he relies on me God. Trump will fight for babies born or not born yet, and he will also try to put me, God back into the American classroom because he loves children. I have given Trump behavior characteristics similar to mine, Enjoy Trump's presidency and pray for the upcoming president after him, that he will know me personally also, so this country can be blessed.

Jan. 27, 2025

In many ways, many Americans will be saved and return to me, God. And America will stay the leading nation of the world.

www.ingramcontent.com/pod-product-compliance
Lightning Source LLC
Chambersburg PA
CBHW042239140626
46547CB00036B/66